Wasting Disease

New Women's Voices Series, No. 153

poems by

Amanda Gomez

Finishing Line Press
Georgetown, Kentucky

Wasting Disease

New Women's Voices Series, No. 153

Copyright © 2020 by Amanda Gomez
ISBN 978-1-64662-328-0 First Edition
All rights reserved under International and Pan-American Copyright Conventions. No part of this book may be reproduced in any manner whatsoever without written permission from the publisher, except in the case of brief quotations embodied in critical articles and reviews.

ACKNOWLEDGMENTS

Grateful acknowledgement is made to the following journals in which some of the poems, at times in different forms, first appeared: *Academy of American Poets (online)*, *Nimrod International Journal*, *North American Review*, *PANK*, *Tupelo Quarterly*, *Switchback*, *BlazeVOX*, and *Madison Review*.

My deepest appreciation to Sundress Academy for the Arts for the opportunity to revise and edit this chapbook and to my mentors Luisa A. Igloria and Tim Seibles for their guidance, mentorship, and encouragement. Additional thanks to Finishing Line Press and Leah Maines for this wonderful opportunity.

And to my family. Most importantly, my mother. While many may see this book as a story of pain, this is a love letter to the little histories we've buried.

Publisher: Leah Huete de Maines
Editor: Christen Kincaid
Cover Art: Melissa Imari Alvarez
Author Photo: Joseph Hyde, Golden Capture
Cover Design: Elizabeth Maines McCleavy

Order online: www.finishinglinepress.com
also available on amazon.com

Author inquiries and mail orders:
Finishing Line Press
P. O. Box 1626
Georgetown, Kentucky 40324
U. S. A.

Table of Contents

Wasting Disease 1

Roadkill 2

Shopping Spree: An Elegy 3

Dreaming of Warriena Wright 4

Grind 5

Codependency: A Fairy-tale 6

Pomegranates 8

Autopsy of My Mother 9

Confession 10

Lessons on Bilingualism 11

Do You Ever Write Translations? 13

Rita Moreno Re-Wears 1962 Oscar Dress 14

Prayer 15

Sometimes it's Necessary to Bury Sweetness 17

Offering 21

On Heartbreak 22

Notes 23

Wasting Disease

after Marilou Awiakta

Little girls dissolve like starfish: their waterlogged limbs
    sprawled across the shoreline.

It's difficult to tell—which are sand flecks and which
    the remnants of skin.

"It's a horror show" scientists say. First, white lesions
    appear. Then, *limb by limb*

their bodies turn limp. Sometimes, an arm twists and falls.
    On rare occasion, bodies melt

into a kind of paste. I guess what I am saying is, every girl
    learns to disintegrate.

Roadkill

They're everywhere. No one mentions it. They don't
have to. I know you inhabit every carcass. I'm running

for what seems like hours. I do my best not to trample
their bodies. Without a clearing, there's no way to know

when this ravaging ends. It smells like piss and rotten figs.
I hold my breath so as not to taste it. Too afraid stench

will slip its fingers between my lips. Clamber inside
to puncture my tongue. I'm running still. Feet blistered.

My toes capped in blood. I buried something somewhere
along this trail of rotting flesh and bones. It's a devastation

I can't recall. Please, if you find out how to retrace your steps
in a dream, tell me. I was told it looks something like communion.

Shopping Spree: An Elegy

    Laughing at a joke,
       something most people do,
    a co-worker tells me:
        You sound like a cheerleader.
  Excuse me? I ask.
You know. *You're just all bubbly and peppy*, she says.
    And it's not that she's calling me a cheerleader
       but *cheerleader*
    in that something in my laugh says
        superficiality, shallowness, the fake
  bitch that talks behind your back.
    Some trope fashioned

        from airbrushed movie actresses,
          Playboy pics,
fucking teen girl trends in ads for Abercrombie & Fitch,
      or watching Jennifer Love Hewitt's
      Conan interview where she's all smiley
         encouraging other girls
    to vajazzle their pussies.
     It's like a sparkly secret in your pants, she says,
    her skin all clear and glittering
       under studio lights.
        She's all bronzer and waist
   expanding the distance
 between feminine expectancy
      and reality.
    So thinking of my co-worker's reaction—
the joke pandering insult,
      she's not the only one, I'm sure, thinking:
     Do I always need to worry about my looks?
Will it always be like this?
     Will I always have to _____?

Dreaming of Warriena Wright

Growing up, my best friend's mom told us stories
about wife-beating husbands, strangled corpses,
and child abductions. It didn't help much either
her husband was a cop. He kept her up to date
with the latest crime patterns where we lived: *Always
have your keys in hand when walking to the car*
she'd say. Or: *If you're in a bad part of town stopped
at a red light, don't wait for it to turn green.
Just drive through. You're a sitting duck if not.*
But the craziest advice was when she told us
that if a man ever wrangled us into his car, to rip off
a button, assuming we had one, and put it in the ignition
that way the key wouldn't fit, assuming we wouldn't be
tied up or locked in the trunk, assuming the button fit the slot.
So naturally, when I left home I binge-watched shows
like *Law and Order: SVU* and *Snapped*. One night,
lying on the couch, I caught a *60 minutes* episode
about a Tinder date gone wrong. Warriena Wright,
a girl my age, was trapped on a 14th floor balcony.
Trying to escape her date, she attempted to climb
over the rail, reach the neighbor below. But drunk,
she slipped and fell. Technically, yes, he didn't kill her,
but if that's the last resort to safety, it might as well
be murder. The best part: he recorded the entire night:
his phone tucked in his chest pocket. When asked
by the reporter why he would to do such a thing, he said:
*I can't remember what happens when I drink. I was protecting
myself in case she made a false claim of rape.* What
he doesn't say: he gave her a red necklace with his hands.
At the morgue, they found a snip of her jeans
lodged in her skull: evidence her body bent
in half, as if she hugged herself mid-air to reach
the safest place she could before death.

Grind

> *for Rita Moreno*
> *West Side Story, 1961*

In the drugstore taunting scene, before Anita lies
about Maria's death - we forget Rita's painted face:

forget, in this movie, Puerto Ricans are only
dark-skinned—we're silent—run, we think—

hoping she'll escape, as the boys, catlike, claw
her skirt—grind her back against cement, leaping

around her legs as fast as light bulbs burn out.
That they will rape her is understood—

not just because she's had sex, or is thought to be oversexed—
but that some women were built as fodder for violence,

their innocence taken hostage. Later,
Rita would admit how the past came knocking

at her throat, how it bruised her soul. How, she too,
was almost raped. *I was filled with every terrible rage*

she says, *when I said the line, "Don't you dare touch me"*:
her jaw a sharp arrangement of bone, as if to say,

this is the hurt we sew inside our ribs,
cutworked, patterned: a trauma set in place.

Codependency: A Fairy-tale

At night, when I can't sleep I repeat   words like:
     enabler,
         caretaker.   Compose inventories of

relationships,
     sexual history. I repeat
           their names. Recite

each one in order:
     my own rosary. Penance
            for my impurity.

Really it's all pretense.   I could grow accustomed
     to this lying.
         Don't we all turn lovers

into spectators?
     I stopped pretending
I know anything about love.

   Recently,
         I told a friend, who I wonder
     is really a friend,

         to pack his stuff. Move out.   It's been days
         and already, I want him gone.
Now   at night anytime

        I flip my light on he peers
                through my door crack to check
if I'm okay. He thinks

            this is an act   of care. At the core of it,
        he wants to justify his worth
until my resolve

        is wet silt and I'm only a series
of landslides and cavings. As if I'll change
my decision   with even the slightest gesture

of tenderness. He knows I desire notice:
        the need to be inescapably   remembered. I learned
                to love like this.

Pomegranates

It is not yet summer, the season of broken bones and firecrackers, and three teenagers are popping wheelies over makeshift cinder block and plyboard ramps. My father and I are walking around our neighborhood. Around us, a cicada's song drills its melody into the wind, and somewhere the smell of hot dogs cooking pushes past backyard fences. "If we walk this loop twice, we will have walked two miles," he says. I nod as I glance at the horizon. Notice lightning bugs flickering. Their cold light, what has been our trail markers tracking the distance we've traveled so far, thinning under the sharp glow of streetlights. "Why has your mom been giving me such a hard time?" The past month, around ten every morning, she yells at him. Usually, it's never about anything serious. Like how his shoes track dirt across the carpet or how the house is cluttered, to which my father always cites the obvious answer. She doesn't work full-time like him, so she has plenty of time to clean. Besides, he likes his Sundays filled with football and mowing the grass. The only workout he's been consistent with lately. And what I think she means to say, every time she yells his name, is "Get off your lazy ass and help me." Of course, I don't tell him this. I slow my pace. We don't have much time left to talk before we reach our doorstep, where she is most likely waiting. Sensing this, my father quickens his pace; his shoes like hummingbirds knocking against the pavement—how all at once he wants to continue discussing the topic and avoid it. "I know she's upset." He admits, "When I was in Florida, I went to a banquet for work. Some co-worker took a picture with this woman's arm resting on my shoulder, and she saw it. She thinks I was flirting or that lady wouldn't have done that, but I was just being polite." And what am I to say? I'm just fourteen. "I don't know dad. Maybe she's just tired," is all I manage to reply. I can't tell him how lately her eyes are dark pomegranates.

Autopsy of My Mother

In the dream when my mother dies, I am the coroner
    wheeling her into the exam room to split

her chest. I cut a y-shaped slit that curves underneath
    her breasts, separate tissue and skin,

exposing the ribs the way a parent might pull back
    the covers before tucking the child in bed.

Then, just like that I crack her sternum. Pluck
    her heart like a strawberry from its stem:

clipping its cone-shaped body from the cursive stalk.
    Her pulse beating against my skin:

a horde of horses scaling the ridges
    of my hands. Why is it

I've dreamt this dream so many times?
    What holds my attention is not her body

so much as my steady grip; my indifference
    towards the fact of her death. My mother:

a stranger, a study in wounding. Starved for understanding
    I continue to cut, drawing the scalpel from stomach

to pubis region. I scoop what's left from the bowl
    of her pelvis until it's empty. I want to crawl

into it as if it were a cradle, where perhaps, she'd hold me
    the way I always wished.

Confession

Some days loneliness is a lightning bolt
who carves his name in my bedroom wall:
the falling plaster between us a cathedral
glass. Then, a body dragging its own tongue.
Everywhere I stare my shadow is running.
It's the closest thing I produce that's permanent—
from where I kneel I think it looks a lot like love.
Again, I am searching for another word.
Today the body is a plumage of desire.
It would burn this house down if it could.

Lessons on Bilingualism

::

God is hungry like this. He stalks
you like a lion-headed man, his matted mane
the burnt yellow of autumn leaves.

You weren't looking for escape.
You were looking for a storm. A wolf's
shadow to kiss. Every darkness
a deer hunted like prey.

::

Tonight, we will braid
                          our bodies
into a rope.

When we finish
                    our mouths
                    will be like coins
      placed
                          on the eyes
            of the dead.

Maybe we all make room
                              to consume
              ourselves.

You say I taste
                like licorice
       and rebellion.

                        Does that mean you taste
        like civilization?

When you kissed me

                                  your lips
       dissolved

into a pair

              of scissors.

                                Their blades
    slipped
                    inside my mouth. Split
        my tongue.

                              Parted
each half
                            like curtains.

::

Language is a vulture that makes
    its nest in the pocket
between my lungs. When I speak Spanish,
    it flaps its wings. My words
come out flat without an accent.

::

My tongue bows
in submission.
It begs
for a miracle.
It says *help me*
when it means
heal me.

Do You Ever Write Translations?

My mouth is a well
where my shadow goes to drown.

I wish it weren't so suicidal. I tell it
to be patient. Isn't the present

always just a little unsatisfying?
When I think about all the men

I've kissed, I also think about the ones
I wish I could. Listen, I am in love

with desire. Water overflows, claiming
the riverbanks for itself. Mostly, I am in love

with excess, wanting a bed made from
touch. I know because I've tried before.

Listen: this isn't a poem about love
as you would have it. This is about holiness,

a tiny pebble placed underneath the tongue.
A prayer can be small. A mouth can be kept.

Rita Moreno Re-Wears 1962 Oscar Dress

I wear the galaxy like a dress: little suns
bending in their own orbit. Their tongues

hammered into darkness *you would think
they would tarnish*. I keep telling myself

everything that is gold stays gold. It took
a while for me to learn down here eclipse

is another word for skin. I'm transparent
in mine. Please, don't take me for tragic.

Nothing attracts prey like it used to.
In certain parts of the world, disease

is a dog cloaked in the sky's marrow. If I
belonged to you, I'd go hungry for myself.

Prayer

West Side Story, 1961

When Tony visits the fire escape,
you can hear Maria's father briefly call out
Maruca, her pet name, affectionate shorthand
for Maria or our Lady of Guadalupe
standing with the baby Jesus on her nightstand
or St. Maria: patron of youth, purity, and victims of rape;
venerated for her aversion to sexual sin. Call her: virgin,
unadulterated gem, our blessed girl. *Say it
slowly and it's almost like praying.* Her name:
an invocation or blessing, so I am left
with the vague interpretation nobody gives
two shits about girls who don't act
like they're supposed to as Tony whispers the lyric
before reaching the alley. Which reminds me of a play
I saw once in high school: three girls standing in a row
with a single rose clasped in their hands
while a man walked around glancing up and down
their bodies. When a girl offered her flower
he'd destroy it. Crumple and crush the petals
with his fists before dropping them on the ground.
Of course, the last girl didn't put out. Her reward:
marriage. I'm sure it was meant to teach us abstinence.
To be disaffected by hormones. I tried to wait. I did.
But when I woke up in my boyfriend's bed and found
an orchid in full bloom on the bed sheets
I gave up. No one questions a man's responsibility
in sex. After it happened, I vowed I'd take whatever I wanted
from men, but reciprocation plays
a fine instrument. Look at me now: empty cunt
like a sock on the street, bastardized version
of what *maruca* really means. A slang or ghetto Spanish
pronunciation of *muñeca* meaning wrist or doll.

What I'd like to think an inside joke which has lost
its punch about how we prefer delicate things. How sensuously
the single r rolls off the tongue. How her name: Maria
is like exhaling stars. Something
like dusty glows prying themselves loose from candle flames.
Like Mother Mary's aureole. The same radiant
luminous cloud shrouding Maria. Watching her bent over,
cradling his head, I wish to be soft as well. Sanctified enough
for a man to look at me like this. But I'm no angel.

Sometimes it's Necessary to Bury Sweetness

West Side Story, 1961

I.

We should worry Anita has a point, sharp-edged
as the belt buckles that bruise
her hips as the Jets tug at her waist. She says
girls here are free to have fun.
Worry when she tells Bernardo to ease up,
let little Maria attend the dance.
We know what Anita's really saying is girls
can have sex whenever
they want. After all, what could it hurt?
She is in America now.
And we know she's right. We should worry
when we don't see her again
after she's raped; worry the film is faithful
to the narrative of brown girls.

II.

There's always this: the narrative of brown girls.
Their bodies: bedrock too rough for men to rest
their heads. Would you believe me if I told you I want
nothing of comfort? Today, I am a girl the world
forces to swallow rain. Before a date shifts the car in gear
to drive me home, he unzips his pants. Tells me
the least I can offer him is a hand job. Instead, I do
what he doesn't ask, I put him in my mouth.
I thought I had to to get home. It sounds crazy now,
but I didn't know I had an option. After I finish
he takes a pen from his center console. Writes *IOU*
on my left arm. Kindness is a luxury. Once a woman
is assaulted, chances of it happening again are higher.

III.

The chances of it happening again are exponentially higher
especially considering the fact that at least one in three Latinas
experiences sexual violence. Just look at my family. I'm 26
when my mother finally tells me she was molested. I'm 26
when I finally tell her I was molested. *Your grandmother too*
my mother adds later in the conversation. Little histories
we've buried from each other. When I unearth them,
a beehive blooms from the dirt like a flower. I eat
a spoonful of its nectar. I call out for someone to share it with
but no one answers. Don't tell me destruction
is beautiful like that. Grandmother, mother, daughter
fragments of each other, fragments of our bodies.
I ask her what would've happened if we ever talked about it, but really,
it doesn't matter. *I can't tell you* mama answers.

IV.

I can tell you one thing, mama says
during the bridal shop scene in *West Side Story* just before
the dance, in the original script Anita tells
Maria: *With those boys you can start in dancing and end up
kneeling.* Some say it's all about marriage:
kneeling before the altar knocked up, but mama disagrees.
She tells me: *they're not talking about praying*
even though Anita says this in the movie. No, it's sex.
Once, when I was younger I remember
a friend's advice on how to give better head: *it's all about
eye contact* she said. Not just submission,
but the act of relishing it. Maybe Auden was right—*The terminal
point of addiction is damnation* and I was a girl
burning in a fire of my body's making.

V.

I was a girl burning in a fire of my body's making. I'm afraid
that all I know is how to talk about loss.
For instance, some studies state Latinas are more at risk for eating
disorders. Mostly if they're 2nd generation.
For me, I was eight. On vacation, I told my parents I liked
to throw up. Then, at sixteen a cousin pinched
my arm fat and said: *This needs to be gone next time you visit,*
so I decided to stop eating so much.
When he saw me, a friend's dad praised my success: *See,*
sometimes all you need is to close your mouth.
At the time, I weighed twenty pounds less than now. I am a mirror
of everything I don't want, an entrance
for others' desires. In a dream, I am a python bathing in a swamp.
In a dream, there is no Eden, no Eve.

VI.

I mistook a swamp for Eden. There is no Eve. Only a dream
where my stomach is a clump of worms nesting
in the ground. I make my bed on snakeskins and scorpion hooks:
cathedral of the misinterpreted. I wake
in a mango grove where the fruit is pallored and bruised,
shaken in the wind like trout fish writhing
on the end of a lure. The gauze of their scales wrapping
my limbs. I'm close to desiring darkness.
I'm a coward; a massacre of wanting. Every word
I speak is a woman on the roadside lifting her dress.
An act in obtaining permission. This language
does not belong in my mouth. I am a skeleton
of honey. Yes, sometimes, it's necessary to bury sweetness.

VII.

Sometimes it's necessary to bury sweetness.
To mistake your lover's skin for a salt mine. Once
a Vietnam veteran told me: *You could always tell
the soldiers who just came in from their marches. Their pants
speckled with white patches.* Salt gems
from the sweat gathered in the folds of their clothing. We're standing
on the stairs leading to his basement. The walls:
draped in memory. *This is one of the rare occasions he's talked
about what happened,* his wife tells us as he sheds
his silence the way a rattler removes its skin. All that is bitter:
a watermark, a hymn of rain. Maybe this is why
when I imagine an alternative ending for Anita, I see her
leaping across a horizon of fire escapes. Her body
a forked tongue rising like a canary remembering song.

VIII.

Like a forked tongue rising as a canary remembering song,
I am not real. I am imagined. There is no such thing
as alternative endings, so forgive me if I don't believe it
when I attempt to rewrite Anita's ending.
I don't have time for false hope. My body is written
into your history. If I am erased
I will be the one to do it. I will erase Anita too. And I will follow
the Western scripts. I will play the sexpot, the Latin
lover. I'll wear my accent thick as a fur scarf around my throat.
I'll come close to strangling myself
but not before you laugh. I promise I can make that happen.
And when I'm done playing maid
or bank robber, you'll call me beautiful or tragic.
you won't see the sharp-edged shiv in my hand.

Offering

April and a morning shower blankets us, covers
the shed out back where my father's fishing equipment
is stored. On mornings like this, he searches
beneath rain gutters for worms loosening the earth
with his hands, sifting it back and forth; collecting
each body he finds in old crusted Tupperware for bait.
Sometimes, when there isn't enough, he cuts them
in half. How concerned he is, ensuring there's enough.
It's the silence he likes: the solace of being alone,
standing on the bank holding his fishing rod, watching
nothing but the tug of the line against the current until a fish
takes the bait. Most days when he brings home a good catch
I like to watch my mother clean the fish. I stand
by the kitchen sink staring at her blood-covered hands
as she tugs their heads backwards, stripping
the skin from its flesh: this new kind of nakedness.

On Heartbreak

In Marina Abramović's *Portrait
with a Scorpion*, the arthropod spreads
its legs across her face, extending
from brow to nasal ridge in magnetic
display; despite the grayscale, the semblance
between creature and woman is more likely
than it seems, her visage a mirror to this
armored thing. It's hardly noticeable,
her emotional state. The stark contrast
so overwhelming. And how does she know
the outcome? A venomous sting,
the unlikelihood of a good ending.
Will she survive or swell up? Succumb
to some inflammatory response?
Will she purge her stomach, retch
all night on her couch? Perhaps this
is what we talk about when we talk about
love: this disgusting fantastic confusion.
We love and fail despite our misgivings.
Perhaps, this is all: this document
and its facing pages, a lesson in scars.

Notes

"Wasting Disease," also known as sea star wasting disease or starfish wasting syndrome, aspires to be in conversation with Marilou Awiakta's poem, "Women Die Like Trees," and borrows the lines "limb by limb."

"Dreaming of Warriena Wright" was inspired by 60 Minutes Australia episode aired on November 13, 2016.

"Rita Moreno Re-Wears 1962 Oscar Dress" borrows language from an interview Rita Moreno gave for E News on the red carpet.

Amanda Gomez is a Latinx poet from Norfolk, VA, where she received her MFA in poetry at Old Dominion University. Some of her poems have appeared in *Nimrod International Journal, North American Review, PANK, Tupelo Quarterly,* and *Writers Resist.*

www.ingramcontent.com/pod-product-compliance
Lightning Source LLC
LaVergne TN
LVHW040118080426
835507LV00041B/1773